Appuldurcombe House

ISLE OF WIGHT

L O J BOYNTON MA, DPhil, FSA
Reader in History, University of London

Appuldurcombe was once one of he most important estates on the Isle of Wight, and was the home of the eminent Worsley family for about 300 years. The house itself was begun early in the eighteenth century by Sir Robert Worsley, and enlarged and altered some seventy years later by his great nephew, Sir Richard. It has been uninhabited since 1909, but although only the shell remains, it is still a beautiful building, and the east front is architecturally important. The grounds were landscaped at the end of the eighteenth century by 'Capability' Brown.

This handbook provides a full history of the house, and begins with a description and tour of the building and grounds.

CONTENTS

Unless otherwise stated illustrations are copyright English Heritage and the photographs were taken by the English Heritage Photographic Unit (Photo Library: 01793 414 903)

Visit our website at www.english-heritage.org.uk

Published by English Heritage
1 Waterhouse Square
138-142 Holborn
London EC1N 2ST
© Crown copyright 1967
Previously published by HMSO 1967
Second edition published by English Heritage 1986,
reprinted 1988, 1990, 1993, 1996, 2001, 2005, 2009
Printed in England by Pureprint Group
05/09, C15, 04026
ISBN 978-1-85074-052-0

TOUR AND DESCRIPTION

The house from the south-east

The present approach to Appuldurcombe is from the north lodge. From there a path leads through the trees to the east front of the house. This is the best starting point for a tour, since the east front is unquestionably the most interesting as well as the most beautiful part of the house. *(A plan of the house is shown on page 16.)*

EAST FRONT

Architectural style

The east front was begun in 1701. At that time the leading English architects were developing their own version of the European style of architecture known as baroque (see Glossary). Since these architects were mostly employed by the government department of the King's Works, it is not surprising that the baroque style in England came to be associated with the Stuarts, the Tories and high-church Anglicanism. After 1714, the coming of the Hanoverians, the Whig political party and more liberal religious views meant that the baroque style went out of fashion. It was superseded by a more orthodox form of classical architecture known as English Palladianism. Appuldurcombe therefore belongs to a short-lived architectural style, English Baroque.

The satyr mask above the east door

In contrast to the later Palladian emphasis on first-floor rooms and windows, the English Baroque tended to treat the two main storeys (excluding the attic) as of equal importance. Appuldurcombe is an example of this. Equally characteristic of the baroque style are the mouldings round the door and windows, and the triple wedge-shaped keystones above the centre of each window. Less common, but also perfectly in period, are the round bull's-eye window and the beautifully carved scrolls, swags of drapery, and the mask of the mythological satyr above the door.

The pavilions

The ends of the building are emphasised by projecting wings or pavilions. This is most unusual for a house of this period. The standard country house of the late seventeenth century, like Belton in Lincolnshire, nearly always had its central section emphasised by a triangular, gable-like, pediment. If it had subsidiary wings, they were not stressed. Here at Appuldurcombe, the pediments are at either end and the doorway, though important, does not dominate the design.

The practice of emphasising the ends instead of the centre of the facade seems to derive from Louis le Vau's mid-seventeenth-century design for the chateau at Vaux-le-Vicomte in France. In England, John Webb's 1662 design for the wing of the Charles II block at Greenwich was duplicated in a design by John James, who thus produced a version of the dual end-pavilions.[1] Talman's design of the south front at Chatsworth House in Derbyshire (begun in 1686) clearly emphasised the two end pavilions, but without the additional stress of pediments.

The north-east pavilion, which contained the dining room

Entrance area

Unlike most of its contemporaries, Appuldurcombe House has no major pediment to emphasise the doorway at the centre of the facade. Instead, the central doorway is emphasised by engaged columns of a 'giant order' - columns attached to the walls and more than a storey high. This was a distinctively baroque feature (though giant orders also occur in the `temple porticoes' of some Palladian houses).

According to the illustration in *Vitruvius Britannicus*[2] (see page 21), there was originally a small pediment above the columns, broken at the top by a scroll-like ornamental panel, or cartouche. The broken pediment and cartouche were baroque features that were considered to be architecturally incorrect during the Palladian period, and were later removed. They may have disappeared as early as 1713, when the builder James Clarke is known to have altered the pediment. The alternate urns and statuettes which appear to have originally crowned the attic (see page 21) were presumably later removed for the same reason.

The walls

The rest of the facade is united vertically by its giant pilasters or shallow rectangular columns, which are topped with Corinthian capitals, separate sections of entablature and a great modillion cornice embracing the entire building (see diagram on page 32). The source for this design may perhaps be traced back to Palladio's Palazzo Valmorana in Vicenza in Italy, but is more likely to have been based on the more recent work of Le Vau at the Tuileries in Paris.[3] The pilasters are of smooth hewn stone or ashlar, and the same finish is used for the horizontal string course that runs round the building below the lower windows. The contrast in texture with the rest of the V--jointed masonry, which has a deliberately rough appearance, is important in keeping the different parts of the design clear. The horizontal style of the design was particularly associated with France, and is quite different from the nearly contemporary work at Dyrham Park in Gloucestershire.

The roof

The pavilions originally showed another French feature. Behind the pediments, the roof was of the mansard type, with a double slope. The marks of its alignment with the attic are visible in the two end-pavilions. The visual awkwardness of the differing outlines of pediment and mansard roof no doubt explains why the roof was later altered. Finally, the chimneys are paired to form triumphal arches. This feature is also found in other buildings by Appuldurcombe's architect, John James, though it is not unique to him.

Comparison with other country houses

Apart from the similarities already described, Appuldurcombe shares certain other features with other country houses built at the same time. The door, for example, may be compared with that of Thoresby in Nottinghamshire (1671). The mask, swags of drapery and triple keystones are similar to those at Drayton in Northamptonshire (1702). Projecting ends, Corinthian pilasters, and niches similar to those in the east front appear on the south front of Barnsley Park in Gloucestershire. The resemblance in this case is particularly interesting, for Barnsley Park was built for Henry Perrot, who had married the first Duke of Chando's niece, and Appuldurcombe's designer, John James, was employed by the Duke in 1714 for his mansion at Canons in Middlesex.[4] It may be that James was connected with all three houses.

SOUTH FRONT

The south front needs less comment. It shows work of two periods. The pavilions and the wall connecting them are early eighteenth-century, contemporary with the east front. The colonnade of arches surmounted by a cast-iron balustrade, together with the stone path, are of the Yarborough period (see page 27).

THE HALL

The hall, entered directly from the east front, has several interesting features. It was originally only one room deep, that is, its west wall was an outside wall. Evidence for this may be seen in the blocked windows and keystones of the cellar windows beneath the west wall, which are obviously exterior features.

The original ceiling of the hall was evidently quite low. It was raised in the 1770s, as can be seen from the later joist holes above the columns. When the ceiling was raised, the fireplaces on the first floor also had to be raised, and indeed the proportions of the upper rooms were sacrificed to improve the ground floor. The columns, which were added at the same time, are made of scagliola, a composite material made to imitate, in this case, the rock porphyry, and were topped by Ionic capitals and frieze.

The marble floor was laid at the same time. The patterns in the north and south doorways, which appear to be off centre, suggest that the original segmental-headed doorways were re-aligned, and doubtless replaced by rectangular doors in the Adam manner. The south end was partly restored in 1987.

SOUTH RANGE

The south-east pavilion contained the drawing room. Behind this was the library, a long room formed out of three smaller rooms in the 1830s. The library once housed part of Appuldurcombe's art collection. Structural remains suggest that the original grand staircase was here, near the present cellar steps.

Immediately adjoining the library and the hall is the only surviving staircase, which has cast-iron railings in a debased Adam style. From the stairs, some of the blocked hall windows can be seen. One of these bears the date 1776, scratched in the rendering by a workman.

From here, ante-rooms lead to the north-east pavilion, and to the service quarters. These rooms were added during the alterations of the 1770s, which made the accommodation larger yet more compact.

NORTH RANGE

The north-west pavilion, which contained the kitchen, was apparently built only in the 1770s, and its masonry is inferior to that of the others. Its foundations were constructed on blue gault clay, which made a major reinstatement necessary when the shell was later restored. At the front of the house, on the north-east pavilion, there are some buttresses against the hall block, which probably indicate that the layer of clay under this side of the house caused problems. The dining room was here in the north-east pavilion.

THE PARK AND GROUNDS

The house, especially perhaps now in its ruination, owes much to the attractiveness of its surrounding grounds. The religious orders who first occupied the site doubtless mostly appreciated it for its seclusion and for the shelter provided by the downs to the west and north. To later owners, these same downland slopes provided a magnificent natural amphitheatre cradling the house and offering ample scope for

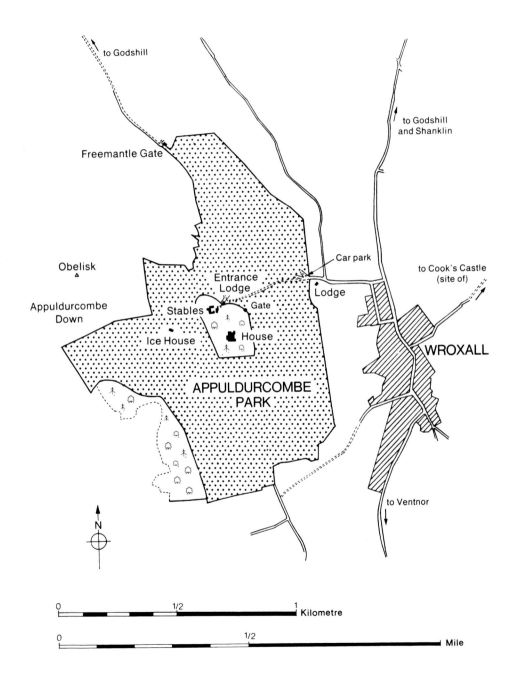

Appuldurcombe Park, an engraving of 1780 by William Watts

improvements to the immediate landscape, while the summits of the downs were marked by viewpoints.

Not all of Sir Robert Worsley's energies were devoted to the rebuilding of the house, but few references survive to his work on the grounds. His brother Henry, resident in Portugal, probably sent him plants, while in 1717 planting was described as his 'reigning folly'. But money was to run out and it was left to Richard Worsley, grandson of his cousin, to undertake a grand reorganising of the grounds.

Richard Worsley (1772-83) returned to Appuldurcombe from a Grand Tour in 1772, determined to complete the house and lay out the grounds in the most fashionable style. He lost no time in employing the celebrated Lancelot 'Capability' Brown. By skilful planting, the use of serpentine drives to create the illusion of size and the construction of 'eye-catchers' on the tops of the downs, Brown transformed the surroundings of the house. His scheme had nearly all the ingredients considered necessary by the late eighteenth-century craving for the natural and the unexpected. Gone were earlier generations' formal ordered gardens and parks; in their place a landscape seemingly evolved by nature but in reality meticulously planned in such a way that the whole could not be seen from any one part and the eye was continually being delighted by fresh and unexpected views.

In the 200 years since Brown's work, changing fashions, neglect, natural regeneration and modern farming have combined substantially to modify the landscape. But clumps of his trees remain, notably in front of the house and on the approach to the Freemantle Gate from Godshill.

Visitors may notice that there are no classical temples, such as usually graced landscaped parks, nor are there lakes and serpentine streams which were equally standard consituents, omissions perhaps the results of economy and the sloping unwatered site. However, the summits of the downs to the east and west were marked by 'eye-catchers' and viewpoints. Nothing survives of the mock-gothic Cook's Castle[5] on St Martin's Down in front of the house, but on the summit of Stenbury Down to the rear is the base of a tall stone obelisk. This was erected in 1774 as a monument to the house's builder, Sir Robert Worsley. It was damaged by lightning in 1831 and it is said that, when Appuldurcombe was later a school, the boys brought away pieces of Cornish granite. Certainly such pieces until recently lined the side of the drive to the rear of the house. In 1984 they were restored to the obelisk.

At the northern end of the former park on the crest of the hill stands the

The Freemantle Gate

Freemantle Gate controlling the approach from Godshill. Reputedly designed by the architect James Wyatt, its fine Ionic triumphal arch and wrought iron gates are chiefly evocative of the past glories of the estate, just as the obelisk and castle were intended to remind the eighteenth-century spectator of past family and national history and the groves of trees were to recall classical art and literature.

Immediately to the north of the house is the site of the demolished domestic buildings, including a laundry and brewhouse. These are now defined by hedges. Beyond this, a lodge and stables can be seen near the entrance gate.[6] The hill-top obelisk was once approached by a serpentine path starting behind the stables and winding past the eighteenth-century ice-house. The latter, now neglected and isolated in a bramble thicket in the field, once stored blocks of ice collected in the winter. Space inside the ice-house was used to keep perishable foods such as fish, butter and meat fresh in the summer, while the ice itself was invaluable for cooling drinks.

When the first Baron Yarborough (1805-55) took control of the estate, he left the park much as Brown had conceived it. But he modified the immediate grounds surrounding the house. He formed the existing boundaries of stone wall, ha-ha and iron railings and constructed the circular fountain in front of the house. Shrubs and a network of paths largely completed his work here.

After the estate was sold in 1855, little was done to maintain or improve park and grounds. The remains of tennis courts bear witness to its use as a boys' school. Since 1980, a programme of estate management has begun, based on extensive historic research. Its aim is to recreate in a simplified and hence more manageable form the immediate surroundings of the house as they would have existed in the first half of the nineteenth century.

HISTORY OF APPULDURCOMBE

EARLY HISTORY

Before the Norman Conquest, the Appuldurcombe estate was part of the manor of Wroxall, which belonged to King Harold's father, the powerful Earl Godwin. In 1086, Wroxall belonged to William the Conqueror, which may explain why Appuldurcombe does not appear in the Domesday Book.

Shortly after Domesday was compiled, the estate was granted to Richard de Redvers, lord of the island. In 1090, he gave it to the Norman Abbey of Montebourg, which established a dependent priory at Appuldurcombe. This priory had an unsettled history. In Richard II's reign, it was looted by French and Spanish raiders. Then, during the French wars of Edward I and Edward III, because it was part of a French religious order, it was forced on more than one occasion to move to the mainland, or allow its affairs to be controlled by the King. Like other foreign religious houses, it was suppressed in 1414.

The King subsequently granted the priory to a group of nuns known as the nuns minoresses without Aldgate. In 1498 the nuns leased it to Sir John Leigh, his wife Agnes, and her son John Fry. The Leighs' daughter Anne married Sir James Worsley, who obtained a new lease. After the Dissolution of the Monasteries, Sir James gained outright possession of the property, thus bringing it into the Worsley family.[7] The estate at that time comprised the manors of: Appuldurcombe, Stenbury, Nettlecombe and Wath, Whitwell, Chale and Walpan, Woolverton and Clavells; and it included property in the parishes of Newchurch, Sandford, Week, Witcombe, Godshill, Whitwell, Stenbury, Nettlecombe, Wath, St Lawrence, Chale, Walpan, Brading, Bembridge, Woolverton, Whippingham and Arreton.

For the next three hundred years, Appuldurcombe was the seat of the Isle of Wight Worsleys. Some of them lived quietly on their estates and made no mark. Others were eminent in local or national affairs. Two were outstanding: Sir Robert, who built the present house, and Sir Richard, who modified the house and also became a nationally famous collector.

THE WORSLEYS OF APPULDURCOMBE

What makes a family like the Worsleys flourish or decline? To find out, it is always worth studying the family history to see what kind of people they were and what marriage-alliances they made.

The Worsley family originated in Lancashire. From it branched the Worsleys of Hovingham in Yorkshire, and the Worsleys of Appuldurcombe.

The Worsleys in Tudor times

In the sixteenth century, James Worsley, like so many of his contemporaries, made his way by attracting royal favour. He became a page to Henry VII, and was brought up with the King's son who, on his accession as Henry VIII, knighted his friend Worsley and appointed him as Keeper of the Wardrobe. In 1511, he gave Worsley a virtual monopoly of official posts in the Isle of Wight, including those of sheriff and coroner, the constableship of Carisbrooke Castle and, most important of all, military captaincy of the island. Worsley then married Anne Leigh, the heiress of Appuldurcombe (the fine altar tomb of her parents, and a monument to Sir James and herself with several other family memorials, are in Godshill Church), and thus consolidated his interest in the island. At his death in 1538, he bequeathed his best gold chain to Henry VIII, and his largest standing cup or goblet to the King's chief servant, Thomas Cromwell.

James was succeeded by his son Richard, who is said to have entertained the King and Thomas Cromwell at Appuldurcombe. The Holbein portrait of Henry which remained there until 1855 was said to have been given by the King at that time. The main purpose of such a visit must have been to inspect the local defences, since war with France was imminent. Indeed, in 1545, Richard led the resistance to a French attack on the island. He built a number of forts here, at Portsmouth, and in the Channel Islands.

Richard also acted as a commissioner for the sale of church property during the Reformation of the Church. As a consequence, he had to lie low during Mary's brief reign, when Catholicism was restored. When the Protestant Elizabeth I came to the throne, she reinstated Richard. He died in 1565, however, and two years later, both his sons were killed by an explosion in the gatehouse at Appuldurcombe when a spark ignited gunpowder that was drying in preparation for a military exercise.

Richard was therefore succeeded by his brother John, who held the estate until 1580. His son Thomas was still a minor, and a ward of Queen Elizabeth's principal secretary, Sir Francis Walsingham. Five years later, Thomas married Barbara, daughter of William St John of Farley in Hampshire.

Marriage was, of course, one of the chief means by which gentry families could rise in society, for brides normally brought dowries and, almost as valuable, connections. Thomas's marriage was the first of an important series of Worsley alliances - to the St Johns, Nevilles, Wallops, Herberts and Thynnes. Since

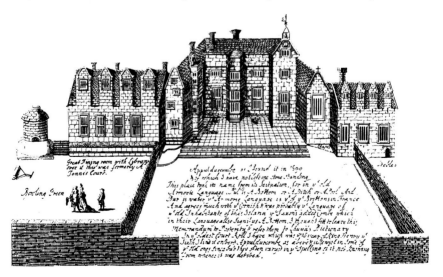

The Tudor house at Appuldurcombe, from Sir Richard Worsley's History of the Isle of Wight

Sir William St John's grandfather was a half-nephew of Lady Margaret Beaufort, mother of Henry VII, the marriage brought a connection, albeit distant, with the royal house of Tudor.

The first baronets

When Thomas Worsley died in 1604, he was followed by his son Richard who, in 1611, was created a baronet by James I only a month after that rank was established. Of Richard's marriage to Frances Neville of Billingbeare in Berkshire, his neighbour Sir John Oglander remarked, 'I think fancy prevailed over portion'. Nevertheless, the Neville's family connections included Queen Elizabeth's great minister, Lord Burghley.

Richard's son Henry succeeded him in 1621. He married Bridget, daughter of Sir Henry Wallop of Farleigh Wallop near Basingstoke in Hampshire. Henry acquired the manor of Chilton Candover in Hampshire, which remained an additional Worsley seat until 1747. Henry's younger son James lived at Pilewell in Hampshire.

Sir Henry was succeeded by his elder son Robert. Robert married Mary, daughter of the Hon James Herbert of Tythrop, in the parish of Kingsey, Buckinghamshire, second son of the fourth Earl of Pembroke, who had been parliamentary governor of the Isle of Wight. Mary Herbert's pedigree was particularly interesting. It included the poet Sir Philip Sidney, the Earl of Leicester, Queen Elizabeth's favourite, Ann Parr, the sister of Henry VIII's last queen, the Earl of Oxford, another of Elizabeth's courtiers, and Anne Cecil, Lord Burghley's daughter.

The Worsleys at their peak

Sir Robert had two sons, of whom the younger, Henry, was, like so many of his family, addicted to travel. He often ventured far beyond the conventionally visited countries, and his tours of the Mediterranean in 1701-2 took in Cyprus, Palestine, Tripoli and Egypt. It is not surprising that Henry later became envoy to Portugal, and Governor of Barbados. It is less predictable that he should also have been a keen antiquary and a member of the Royal Society.

The elder son, Robert, succeeded his father at the age of seven. On coming of age in 1690, he married the Hon Frances Thynne, daughter of the first Viscount Weymouth of Longleat. At this point, it is interesting to note that none of the Worsley marriages had roamed beyond the counties of Hampshire, Wiltshire, Berkshire and Buckinghamshire. Just as landowners always tried to consolidate their estates in one part of the country to enable them to be managed more efficiently, so the Worsleys seem, at any rate until well into the eighteenth century, to have kept their marriage-alliances within useful range.

Sir Robert followed his brother Henry as MP for Newtown, Isle of Wight, and like him was a loyal supporter of the Whigs, who came to power in 1714. Though he spent part of each year in London, Robert was more interested in his country estates at Chilton Candover and at Appuldurcombe, where he started to rebuild the house and to lay out new gardens. In 1717 he admitted to Henry, who sent him rare plants from Portugal, that planting was his 'reigning folly', and gardening remained one of his chief amusements all his life.

Through his wife, Sir Robert inherited the famous Essex ring and a lock of the hair of Elizabeth's favourite (now in Westminster Abbey and Ham House respectively), and the fifteenth-century Bedford Book of Hours, now one of the principal manuscripts in the British Museum. The couple's intellectual friends included Bishop Ken and the satirist

Jonathan Swift, and the writing box which Lady Worsley japanned or lacquered for Swift is still at St Patrick's Deanery in Dublin. Sir Robert's daughter reinforced the Whig connection by marrying the powerful Lord Carteret, George II's favourite minister, whose influence undoubtedly helped the Worsleys.

This brilliant chapter in the family's history was to be followed by an anti-climax, however, because Sir Robert's sons died before he did. The property at Chilton Candover was bequeathed to Carteret's son and the baronetcy and Appuldurcombe passed to Robert's cousin, Sir James Worsley of Pilewell.

Sir Robert's will directed that 'nothing of mine at Appuldurcombe except the plate shall be sold or removed, but remain there as heirlooms and go with the possession and inheritance of Appuldurcombe for ever'. His brother Henry had likewise left his considerable library to the owner of Appuldurcombe for the time being 'as long as the same shall continue to be enjoyed by any descendants from the family of Worsley'. There could be no clearer expression of the strong feeling of family continuity which it is so necessary to understand when considering the building of a house such as Appuldurcombe.

The Worsleys of Pilewell
When James Worsley of Pilewell succeeded to his cousin Sir Robert, Pilewell took the place of Chilton Candover as an alternative residence to Appuldurcombe. All that need be said about Sir James, the fifth baronet, is that he shared the family's antiquarian interests, and collected material towards a history of the Isle of Wight, which his grandson Richard published in 1781.[8]

James's son Thomas succeeded him in 1756. He was married to Elizabeth Boyle, daughter of the fifth Earl of Cork and Orrery. Sir Thomas devoted much of his time to the South Hampshire Militia, of which he was colonel-in-chief. The young historian Edward Gibbon lived at nearby Buriton and served for a time under Sir Thomas's command when invasion was expected during the Seven Years' War with France. Gibbon's journals, not without a tinge of malice towards his unintellectual, rustic neighbours, imply that Sir Thomas spent much of his time disputing the rights of command with the Duke of Bolton, and most of the remainder in bucolic carousing. Gibbon was not averse to joining in, however, and more than one morning's work was lost as a result.

Sir Thomas kept up the family tradition of travel. In the 1760s he took his family to Sicily when most travellers were content with going as far as Naples.[9]

Rise and fall of the seventh baronet
Thomas was succeeded by his son Richard, who was the last of the family to live at Appuldurcombe. When Richard returned from the family's grand tour in 1772, Gibbon found him not improved. 'From an honest wild English buck, he is grown a Philosopher . . . He speaks in short sentences, quotes Montaigne, seldom smiles, never laughs, drinks only Water, professes to command his passions, and intends to marry in five months.'

The political reformer John Wilkes, who spent a good deal of time at his 'villakin' at Sandham (Sandown), met Sir Richard in August 1772 and thought more kindly of him and his family. After attending church at Shanklin, Wilkes was invited by the Fitzmaurices to Knighton (near Newchurch, now destroyed) where he met Sir Richard and the dramatist David Garrick and his wife. Of Sir Richard he wrote that he 'has a fine seat in the neighbourhood, called Appuldurcomb; where he engaged me to pass Monday, with his mother, sister, &c. Mr and Mrs Garrick, and the set from Knighton, came to a grand breakfast, but did not stay till

*Portrait of Lady Worsley by Sir Joshua
Reynolds, probably painted shortly after her
marriage (Courtesy of the Earl of Harewood)*

*Sir Richard Worsley, wearing the uniform
of his regiment; portrait by Sir Joshua
Reynolds*

dinner. Miss Worsley, a young lady of
fourteen, infinitely engaging, favoured us
with some exquisite songs; and the
company paid her the homage due to such
merit.'[10] Love of music was another family
trait.

Sir Richard succeeded in ingratiating
himself with the government, largely by
operating the parliamentary elections for
the borough of Newton, Isle of Wight, in
its favour. In reward, he was made, among
other things, a privy councillor and
comptroller of George III's household, as
well as governor of the Isle of Wight. He
was less successful in 'drinking only Water'
and controlling his passions, and was
virtually ruined by his disastrous marriage.

In 1775 Sir Richard had married
Seymour Dorothy Fleming ('for love', said
Gibbon, 'and £80,000'). Only seven years
later they parted, following a divorce action
brought by Sir Richard against Captain
Bisset, the last of his wife's admitted
twenty-seven lovers.[11] Sir Richard
miserably failed to win the £20,000
damages he sought - the jury awarded one
shilling on the ground of his connivance.

After the divorce, Sir Richard found it
advisable to give up his position at Court,
and to leave the country for a prolonged
stay in the Mediterranean countries, the
Levant and the Near East. For this reason
also, the magnificent Reynolds
portrait of his wife was banished from

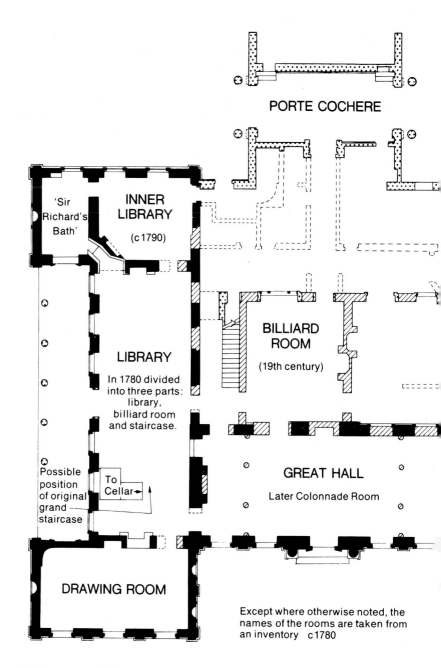

PORTE COCHERE

'Sir Richard's Bath'

INNER LIBRARY

(c 1790)

LIBRARY

In 1780 divided into three parts: library, billiard room and staircase.

Possible position of original grand staircase

To Cellar→

BILLIARD ROOM

(19th century)

GREAT HALL

Later Colonnade Room

DRAWING ROOM

Except where otherwise noted, the names of the rooms are taken from an inventory c1780

Appuldurcombe House, ground floor

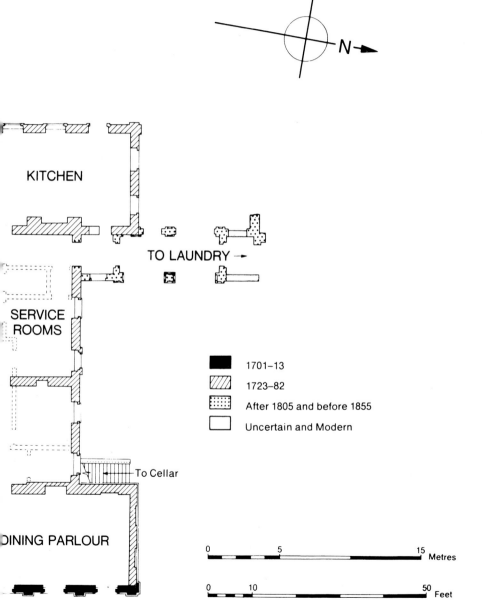

N →

KITCHEN

TO LAUNDRY →

SERVICE
ROOMS

To Cellar

DINING PARLOUR

	1701–13
	1723–82
	After 1805 and before 1855
	Uncertain and Modern

0 5 15 Metres

0 10 50 Feet

Appuldurcombe to the home of her step-father, Edwin Lascelles, at Harewood in Yorkshire. It is now among the best pictures in the gallery there.[12] With the architect Willey Reveley, whose job it was to make architectural and archaeological drawings,[13] Sir Richard spent five adventurous years abroad, often in great danger and hardship. He finally reached Russia, where the political philosopher Jeremy Bentham met (and disliked) him.

The significance of this expedition was that Sir Richard brought back the most important collection of Greek marbles yet seen in England - over twenty years before Lord Elgin shipped his loot from the Parthenon. These were housed at Appuldurcombe, together with a collection of antique gems acquired from Sir William Hamilton. Illustrations of the marbles and gems were published in two handsome volumes known as the *Museum Worsleianum* (1798, 1802). A fine cabinet which housed part of the collection (probably the gems) is now in a private collection in Ireland.

Sir Richard also bought a large assortment of pictures when he was Minister in Venice in 1797, a time when to the normal poverty of many Italian noble families was added fear of the advancing French Revolutionary army. After his return to England in 1797, until his death, Sir Richard continued avidly to buy from the French collections dispersed by the Revolution, and Appuldurcombe became less a house than a museum. At the time of his death in 1805, pictures stood stacked on the floors of some of the rooms at Appuldurcombe. The best pictures, however, were displayed in the main rooms, and visitors were regularly admitted.

Though his collection occupied him until his death, Sir Richard also spent much of his time after 1797 with his 'housekeeper' Mrs Smith, at the more homely Sea Cottage,[14] which is still in existence near St Lawrence Well and is visible from the coast path. Here and in the adjacent house which belonged to his mother, Sir Richard built several classical temples, at least one of which remains. He also planted a vineyard, from which a few straggling vines still survive.

Baron Yarborough

Sir Richard's estates were inherited by his niece, Henrietta. In 1806, she married Charles Anderson Pelham, first Baron Yarborough, whose main seat was at Brocklesby Park in Lincolnshire. Yarborough was the effective founder, and first commodore, of the Royal Yacht Squadron and he kept Appuldurcombe as a convenient base for sailing at Cowes. On the summit of Stenbury Down near the obelisk, he placed a semaphore in order to signal to his yacht.

In 1837 he was created Earl of Yarborough, the Baron Worsley of Appuldurcombe, and the latter title is now held by the heir to the earldom. Yarborough made a few changes at Appuldurcombe, mainly associated with the creation of a library out of three rooms on the south side of the house.

In 1855, the estate was sold, and the best works of art were removed to Brocklesby Park. Many pictures have since been dispersed to private and public collections throughout the world, but some of the best are still at Brocklesby, together with all the antique gems and marbles - except the fifth century BC 'Girl with Doves' which is in the Metropolitan Museum in New York.

AFTER THE WORSLEYS

The house was bought in 1855 by an absentee owner, who in about 1859 leased it to a joint-stock company. The intention was to run it as a hotel, but this venture failed. By 1867, the house had been leased to the Rev Mr Pound, who conducted a 'school or college for young gentlemen' here until the 1890s. From 1901 to 1908, it provided a temporary home for Benedictine monks from the Abbey of Solesmes in France. Harsh anticlerical laws had forced the monks to leave France, and they lived at Appuldurcombe while they were rebuilding Quarr Abbey.

From 1909, Appuldurcombe was unoccupied, except by troops in both wars. In the 1930s there had been a possibility of restoring the house for private occupation, and in 1932 Queen Mary expressed a hope that it might be preserved. But in 1943 a land-mine fell nearby, and hastened the incipient decay by damaging the roof and windows. After the war, the house was in grave danger of being demolished and, commenting on this 'magnificent Queen Anne house', *Country Life* observed that 'existing conditions as a whole make proposals for in some way preserving such a building idealistic'. The magazine went on to suggest that, rather than be demolished, the building should be moved, stone by stone, to a war-damaged city where it could be re-erected.[15]

In the early 1950s a connoisseur of 'picturesque decay' observed that Appuldurcombe had 'disintegrated beautifully in all the morbid shades of a fading bruise'.[16] It was not until 1952 that the decision was taken to preserve it as far as possible. Since then, Appuldurcombe has been in the care of what is now English Heritage (the Historic Buildings and Monuments Commission for England), which has carried out a lengthy programme of repair and consolidation. In 1986, the Great Hall, Drawing Room and Dining Parlour were re-roofed, and their windows replaced. In view of its history over the past half-century, it is not surprising that only the shell remains and there is no 'stately home' to be seen. On the other hand, more of Appuldurcombe's building history is visible now than ever before.

Appuldurcombe in decay, 1954

BUILDING HISTORY

SIR ROBERT'S MANSION 1701-13

In 1690 the twenty-year-old Sir Robert Worsley, the fourth baronet, returned to England from his grand tour of Europe. That same year he secured himself a prominent place in society by marrying Frances Thynne, daughter of the first Viscount Weymouth. The young man's thoughts must then have turned towards building a suitable house as the centre of his estates, and as an expression of his taste and status. His main estates were in the Isle of Wight, and he chose Appuldurcombe for his mansion.

At Appuldurcombe in 1690, Sir Robert found a large Tudor manor house which he drew, or had drawn, as a record of what he was about to demolish (see page 12). His opinion of it may be guessed from his observation 'I have not left one stone standing'. His reasons are easy to see. Not only were such buildings often in bad repair, but they were universally regarded by that time as 'gothic' - that is, irregular and uncivilised from the point of view of both architecture and convenience.

Building commences

The date of the present house has been incorrectly given as 1710 in previous accounts, following Colen Campbell's *Vitruvius Britannicus* and Sir Richard Worsley's *History of the Isle of Wight*. Sir Richard merely remarked that the house was begun in 1710 and left in a 'very unfinished state'. His apparent lack of interest was evidently intended to enhance his own contribution to the building for he wrote: 'it has since been completed by Sir Richard Worsley who has made considerable additions, and very much improved upon the original design'.

In fact, Appuldurcombe was begun earlier than 1710. By 1701 work had started on the north end, and proceeded slowly on the central hall block, the south-west pavilion and the south-east pavilion. However, for financial reasons, Sir Robert left it incomplete.

Finance dictated the speed of building. In 1701 or 1702, Lady Worsley wrote to her father from Appuldurcombe: 'I hope you will find good effect by this fine weather, in recovering your feet [he was gouty] that you may be able to enjoy the pleasure of your garden, which, I guess is now in perfection. We have one no bigger than your parlour that Sir Robert is perpetually in. The Chapell goes up apace. I wish he would let them go on as fast with the rest of the building, that we might see an end of it, which I hardly hope to do'.[17] Her views were no doubt coloured by the fact that she liked London society as much as she disliked that of the Isle of Wight.

Lady Worsley's reference to the 'chapel' is puzzling in a house of such modest size. It may merely refer to rooms in a particular part of the house, for the old house had included secondary bedrooms 'called the Chapel' (the main rooms were called 'Paradise'), and such nicknames remained common in country houses well into the eighteenth century. However, according to Sir Robert's drawing, the old house did have a chapel, and the plain sense of Lady Worsley's letter is that he built a private chapel in the new house. Both of the Worsleys and Lord Weymouth were friendly with Bishop Ken, and it may be that Sir Robert was a devout churchman.

Above the 'chapel' were the best bedroom and a dressing-room, both of which were supplied with fireplaces before

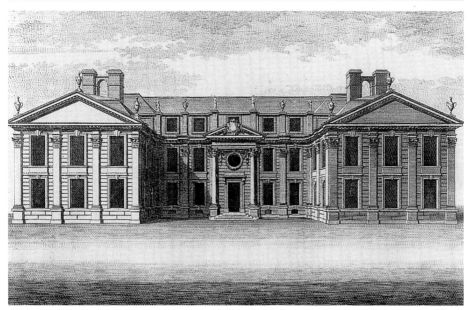

The east elevation of the present house, from Vitruvius Britannicus. *Note the pediment with ornamental cartouche in the centre which originally surmounted the columns, and the urns and statuettes which crowned the attic*

November 1702, and the bedroom with panelling also.[18] In 1703 the Great Storm of 26-27 November, one of the worst ever known in England, badly damaged Appuldurcombe. As a result, Sir Robert had to excuse himself from entertaining the Archduke Charles of Austria (Charles III of Spain), who had sought shelter on the island. Writing to Lord Weymouth, he declared 'my house is only fitt to convince him that the storm has been on shoar as well as at sea, for the old part in the middle is quite stript, & I believe were he there he would not venture under it, & the apartment my wife & I lay in, is not at present to be used, for I built a chimney in the little room next to it just as I came out of the island & the partition could not be finished till spring.'[19]

This mention of the 'old part' shows that the Tudor house was not demolished

before the new one was begun, but that building proceeded piecemeal. There is further evidence for this in the accounts, which in 1704 refer to work 'about the new end of the house'.

The builders
By 1705 the old hall in the centre, which had been cheaply repaired with rough Purbeck stones after the storm, had been demolished. A payment of £321 was made for 'Massens worke about the Hall building in 1705' to William Reynolds and partners, who were evidently responsible for the greater part of the building. In 1705 and 1706 Joseph Clarke was also paid for masonry, and in 1713 James Clarke was paid for altering the pediment above the hall door, in the centre of the east front.[20] Since the Clarkes did comparatively little, it is reasonable to assume that they were

Detail of the east entrance, showing the carved scrolls and swags of drapery and Corinthian capital. This detailing was probably the work of James and Joseph Clarke

engaged on the fine ornamental detail, notably around this central doorway.

The accounts tell us nothing more about these men, but it may be deduced that they were from London. To begin with, Appuldurcombe was the first, and only, house erected in the grand manner in the Isle of Wight, where all previous building had been of a vernacular or local character, like the Tudor house at Appuldurcombe. There can therefore have been no local masons experienced enough to produce work of the quality found on the east and south fronts. It is also likely that the architect (who, as we shall see, was a London man) would have done his best to see that masons he knew were employed on the house. Moreover, masons with the same names - admittedly not very distinctive ones - as those recorded at Appuldurcombe were then flourishing in London.

A Joseph Clarke had become a freeman of the Mason's Company in 1684 and, though neither James Clarke nor William Reynolds appear in the Company's records, Reynolds' partners, John and Thomas Davis, do. It is recorded that a John Clarke became a freeman in 1686, and a Thomas Davis from Winchester, who was Joseph Clarke's first apprentice in 1684 was, like him, a liveryman in 1705. Though the evidence is hardly conclusive, it would be a strange coincidence if there were two groups of Clarkes and Davises at work at the same time.[21]

During 1706, 1707 and 1708 William Reynolds, John Davis and 'young Mr (Thomas) Davis' were at work on Appuldurcombe's south-west pavilion, described as the steward's room wing. It is easy to see why Lady Worsley had been so scathing about the rate of progress, but Sir Robert had bought his grand marriage - alliance dearly, for he had had to settle estates on his wife which, despite her dowry, had led to him being burdened by mortgages.

In 1709 something - probably the general (though misplaced) belief that the War of Spanish Succession was about to end - induced Sir Robert to make a final effort. Reynolds and partners began to build at a faster rate, and in 1711 they reached the south-east pavilion. That year the south-west pavilion was 'healed', that is roofed,[22] and the architect came over to inspect progress.

The architect

So far nothing has been said of the architect, and indeed the building accounts never mention him. He had no doubt produced a design and passed it on to the masons to execute. In the opinion of the historian Arthur Oswald 'he must certainly have been a London man. The building is in the grand manner . . . and it has a sophistication which would be absent from a provincial architect's work. It is by someone well versed in the Wren tradition, who, at the same time, has begun to be influenced by Vanbrugh's baroque compositions.'[23] The same might have been said, however, of a number of architects trained in the King's Works, some of whom, in addition to their official duties, accepted outside commissions.

Sir Robert's letter to his father-in-law Lord Weymouth puts the architect's identity beyond reasonable doubt: 'My stay here will be something longer than I first intended, tho' both that & my comeing, is onely to cover well what I have been 3 years in raiseing, for Mr James's business (who left me last Munday) was to fix the best manner in conveying the water from the roofs.[24] He was much pleased with the Building, as indeed I am allso.' James's name is mentioned on several occasions in letters to Lord Weymouth, and there can be no doubt that he was John James of Greenwich. Indeed in 1711 John James gave Lord Weymouth as a referee.[25]

A key factor in patronage at this time was likely to have been family connection and recommendation. So it is interesting to note that not only did Lord Weymouth back his son-in-law's architect, but the two of them (and Robert's brother Henry and cousin James Worsley) subscribed to John James's translation of Le Blond's *The Theory and Practice of Gardening, Done from the French Original, printed at Paris Anno 1709* (London, 1712). Note also that both Sir Robert Worsley and Mr James Clarke 'Mason' had subscribed to John James's *A treatise of the Five Orders of Columns in Architecture,* which appeared in 1708, translated from the French of Perrault.

John James (born c1672, died 1746) was of Hampshire origin and, indeed, built himself a house there, at Eversley. After 1683 he held various appointments in the King's Works, and in 1718 he was to become, with Nicholas Hawksmoor, joint Clerk of the Works at Greenwich, and sole Clerk in 1736. In 1711 he became Master Carpenter at St Paul's Cathedral, where he was later appointed Assistant Surveyor under the great architect Sir Christopher Wren in 1715 and Surveyor in 1723. His best-known building is probably St George's Church, Hanover Square.

James was clearly a talented man but 'not an architect of genius, and his work is undistinguished in comparison with that of his contemporaries, Gibbs and Hawksmoor'.[26] Now that Appuldurcombe is added to his buildings, however, the assertion that 'he had no sympathy with the Baroque tendencies of the early eighteenth century' needs modification. In 1711 James expressed the opinion that beauty in architecture was proportionate to the plainness of its structure, which has naturally led to his being aligned with the imminent English Palladian revival. If James had designed Appuldurcombe in 1710 or thereabouts (the hitherto accepted date) the expression of such an opinion in 1711 would have needed some explanation. As the house was begun in 1701, however, James had had ample time to change his views by 1711.

The house was not completed by 1711 for reasons which Sir Robert's letter explained: 'but I have done, for I must leave to the next age, both the finishing of this [house], and the paying my own debts & that of the nation, for I see no prospect of its being done in my time. I have been at the labouring oar, ever since I came of age, & must continue so to my grave, & the plenty I remembered in King Charles the 2d's time dureing my minority makes the present prospect appear more melancholy . . .'

Sir Robert was then forty-two, and lived another thirty-six years. If his tone inclines to self-pity, remember that the period since his coming of age had been one of incessant and costly war against France. Moreover, in order to build not only worthily but splendidly, many of the eighteenth-century gentry pinched themselves financially, whereas their nineteenth-century successors tended to pinch their buildings.

Building costs
How much, in fact, did Appuldurcombe cost Sir Robert? The house is mainly constructed of local stone; only the ornamental mouldings and carvings are of Portland stone. Some old stone from the Tudor house was re-used. In 1706, for example, William Reynolds' bill for £331 was reduced by £10, 'an allowance for old hewed stone'.

Local labour, too, provided many materials. John Davis of Borthwood charged £6 for 30 quarters (just under 400kg) of lime used in spring 1702. Planks from a ship - presumably wrecked or salvaged - cost £6 3s 6d for 850ft (259m).

In November 1704 the charge for 1734ft (528.5m) of oak was only £19 11s 0d, and for 500ft (152m) of deal as little as £3 2s 6d. In July 1705 George Hart supplied the masons with six dozen wattles or rods at a cost of £5 8s 0d. In the roofing old lead was allowed against the cost of new, and Richard Harvey bought a piece of mast which was used for shaping the old lead. Sam Smith produced forty deal poles for scaffolding; others brought wattle, lime, hair, gravel, and similar items.

The local stone came from 'Undercliff' on the south-east coast of the island, where the upper Greensand beds of rock provided some good building material. There, a dozen people were employed digging and carting the stone to Appuldurcombe. They were William Reynolds, James Dennett, Richard and Thomas Davis, Ralfe Stone, Eli Butcher, Thomas Hunt, Edward Hardly, Thomas Taylor, Thomas Allen, Thomas Dowding, and the Widow Colman.

The Portland stone was supplied by Mr Deverell and 'Mr Toby' (John Toby, Wren's agent for the supply of Portland stone to St Paul's Cathedral).[27] From Portland, the stone came by sea to Newport or Cowes, and from there Austen Weeks, Matthew Stoner, and Matthew Flower brought it to Appuldurcombe by cart. In all some 280 tonnes were brought, and the freight accounted for £103 out of the stone's total cost of £178. The first shipments arrived in 1705: the carters were rewarded with two hogsheads (large casks) of beer, and the men who supplied beer were given pipes and tobacco.

The progress of the building can be followed from the expenditure, which is shown in the table, as far as it is possible to isolate items. The total recorded expenditure, which amounts to £3532 15s 10d, seems astonishingly small, but there are two comments to be made. First, it is almost impossible to express it in modern terms. Apart from numerous changes in the purchasing power of money, the *scale* of costs in the 1700s was totally

Year	Mason's work	Portland Stone (a)	Local Stone (b)	Interior fittings	Glazing	Plumbing	Roof	Sundries
1702	£183 18 0			£51 8 1				
1703				28 0 10				£13 1 6
1704			£166 4 1	23 14 0				28 15 0
1705	321 5 1 71 7 8(c)	£50 0 8	10 4 8			£157 17 1		7 0 0
1706	221 19 0 124 10 10	63 7 9		13 8 0			£11 13 0	11 0 0
1707	45 10 8		57 11 10		£8 0 0			
1708	236 19 9	15 0 0		9 4 2				29 16 0
1709	277 13 2	22 14 0	226 0 9			30 6 8		26 9 6
1710	268 3 2							
1711	178 19 8	27 11 0	100 8 6			30 15 0(d)	5 7 6	
1712	58 10 0		11 7 0					306 7 9
1713	2 3 4(c)							
Total	£1990 1 4	£178 13 5	£571 17 0	£125 15 1	£8 0 0	£218 18 9	£17 0 6	£422 9 9

Grand total: £3532 15s 10d
(a) including transport
(b) including digging and transport
(c) payment to the Clarkes
(d) part payment of £167 15s 10d. Total was £208 1s 0d but an allowance was made for old lead

Sir Robert Worsley's building accounts for Appuldurcombe

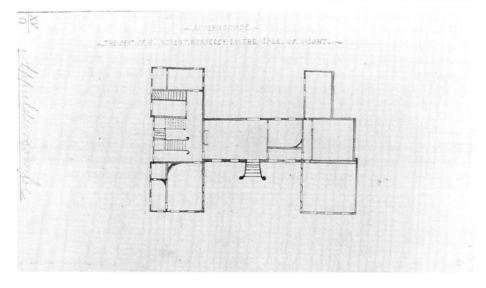

Sketch plan of Appuldurcombe, inscribed 'Appuldurcombe. The Seat of Sir Robert Worsley in the Isle of Wight' (British Museum)

different from today. The low cost of wood has already been mentioned, and note that also 13,000 tiles were bought for only £11 13s 0d in 1706.[28]

Moreover, it is likely that much - no one knows how much - of the materials and labour came from the Worsley estates and, this being so, the cash payment represents only part of the total cost. In any case, the total was not markedly different from the cost of comparable houses. Belton House in Lincolnshire, which is somewhat larger, cost £5091.[29]

The interior

Little is known of the original interior of the house. The sketch-plan (above) is by no means reliable, for it differs from the actual house in several ways. It probably represents a rough preliminary sketch, though the irregular north-west pavilion is hard to accept as such. The spelling 'Applercombe' represents the authentic local pronunciation, though nowadays Appuldurcombe usually has the first syllable (or, regrettably, the third) accented.

The plan as given in the sketch is archaic, with its hall off centre, and its rooms small and inconveniently aligned. The positions of the original joists, still visible in the hall, show that the rooms were not intended to be particularly high. On the other hand, some of the original fireplaces, which were of pink and green marble and were bolection-moulded (with the joints between the different surface levels of the marble skilfully masked by mouldings) were preserved through later alterations because of their high quality, though today neither is at Appuldurcombe. One is now in the entrance hall of Mottistone Manor, and the other is in the old Parsonage, Mottistone. The fireplaces were supplied by 'Mr Fisher, Stonecutter' in 1702, and later by his widow, who received payment in 1706. The cost was £26 18s 0d.[30]

CHANGES 1773-82

Sir Robert, as we have seen, had found himself unable to finish the house he had begun, and left it 'to the next age' to complete. But his sons died before he did, and he was succeeded by his cousin and heir to the baronetcy, Sir James Worsley of Pilewell. Neither Sir James nor his son Sir Thomas showed any sign of interest in the house, and nothing more was done until after Thomas's son Sir Richard had succeeded him in 1768.

Sir Richard returned from his grand tour in 1772, and at once set about completing Appuldurcombe. In his own words, he not only completed and added to, but 'much improved upon the original design'. He built the north-west pavilion and added new rooms and offices to the rear of the hall, thus making the whole plan much more compact. He remodelled the hall and much else in the existing interior, and redecorated in the current style. He also altered the setting of the house to conform to current fashion, and added suitable ornaments. There are apparently no surviving accounts for all these alterations.

Sir Richard was keen to keep up with fashion of every kind. He chose `Capability' Brown as his landscape designer and the celebrated Thomas Chippendale[31] for his furniture, so he probably employed a well-known architect as well. According to Arthur Oswald,[32] the style of the Freemantle Gate in Appuldurcombe Park suggests that it is the work of James Wyatt, one of the eighteenth century's most successful architects. Wyatt therefore may have had a hand in redesigning the interior of the house. Sir Richard's bank account records payments to 'Mr. Wyatt' of £47 11s 0d in 1778 and £100 in 1782.[33] If these refer to *the* Wyatt, it is clear that such sums cannot have covered more than some ideas and advice.

What *is* certain is that the work was carried out under the supervision of William Donn, Donne or Dunn. So little is known about this man's career that it is doubtful whether he should be regarded as an architect in his own right. It may well be that Wyatt recommended Donn to see to the execution of the new designs which were, after all, mainly interior decoration rather than architecture. Sir Richard paid Donn nearly £4000 between July 1774 and March 1782. In addition, individual payments were made to some craftsmen, to Mr Vangilden, for instance, who probably supplied fireplaces. A fine fireplace from the dressing room is now in Fulham Palace.[34]

Donn's position at Appuldurcombe was, no doubt, comparable with the one he filled at Claydon House in Buckinghamshire. There he worked as surveyor or clerk of the works under the architect Sir Thomas Robinson, who accused him of meddling with his plans. In 1771 Robinson quarrelled with Claydon's owner Lord Verney, and Donn took his place. It is interesting to find at Claydon a plan of Appuldurcombe's hall floor (see page 28), which Donn had sent to Lord Verney, presumably as a pattern. Donn wrote to Verney from Appuldurcombe in 1777, and from London in 1782, explaining that business with Sir Richard had prevented his calling.[35]

Some fragments of plasterwork dating from this period have been preserved at Appuldurcombe, and show its fine neo-classical detail. The plasterwork of the library ceiling was executed - somewhat unusually at this time - by Roman craftsmen.[36]

THE YARBOROUGH PERIOD 1805-55

When Sir Richard died, his estates were inherited by his niece, who married Charles

Anderson Pelham, first Baron Yarborough. A guidebook of 1832, describing Appuldurcombe, ominously stated that 'the noble owner is making considerable alterations to the interior of the mansion, which will be entirely remodelled'.[37]

This was an exaggeration, however, for the main change was to the interior on the south side. Here three rooms were reconstructed to form one long room, the library. Alongside the library, a stone path and Roman Doric colonnade surmounted by a cast-iron balustrade were added between the south-east and south-west pavilions. At much the same time the stone basin was erected in front of the east door and at the west door was built a porte-cochère - a porch large enough for wheeled vehicles to pass through.

These were essentially the last of the building improvements at Appuldurcombe. In 1855 the estate was sold, and Appuldurcombe House was never again to be a private residence.

The south-east pavilion, with the stone basin erected by Baron Yarborough in the foreground. Note the chimneys above the pavilion, paired to form a triumphal arch (see page 6)

REFERENCES

1 'The Royal Hospital for Seamen at Greenwich,' *Wren Society* vi (Oxford, 1929), plate XVLI.

2 Colen Campbell, *Vitruvius Britannicus,* iii (London, 1725), 61.

3 See J Marot, *Architecture Françoise* ('Le Grand Marot'), important for its early date-well before Appuldurcombe was built; J F Blondel, *Architecture Françoise* (1756), vo14, liv, vi, no I, pl. 25. I am indebted to Sir John Summerson for these references, for the Vaux comparison, and for much help with the architecture of Appuldurcombe.

4 Christopher Hussey, *English Country Houses: Early Georgian 1715-60* 12, 50.

5 Illustrated in George Brannon, *Graphic sketches of Well-known Subjects in the Isle of Wight* (nd, Wootton, I of W), plate dated 1839 at p 38.

6 See *Wren Society,* iv (Oxford, 1927), passim.

7 The Victoria History of the Counties of England: *Hampshire and the Isle of Wight,* ii (London, 1903), 231-2; v (London, 1912), 171.

8 Sir Richard Worsley, *The History of the Isle of Wight* (London, 1781).

9 I am indebted in this chapter to work done on the family pedigree by Mr P Montague-Smith, editor of Debrett.

10 *The correspondence of the late John Wilkes ...* ed John Almon (London, 1805), iv, 107-8.

11 A transcript of the divorce action is contained in *The Trial (Worsley v Bisset, 1782)* (English Heritage, 1985).

12 Reproduced in Ellis Waterhouse, *Painting in Britain, 1530 to 1790* (London, 1954), pl.138.

13 Reveley's Watercolours of the Temple of Neptune at Paestum and of Reggio, Calabria, are reproduced in Martin Hardie, *Water-colour Painting in Britain* (1966), figs 170-171.

14 Illustrated in George Brannon, *Vectis scenery* (Wootton Common, I of W. 1832, 1842), plate dated 1827.

15 *Country Life,* vol 98 (July-Dec 1945), p 721.

16 Rose Macaulay, *Pleasure of Ruins* (London, 1953), p 454.

17 Thynne MSS at Longleat House, Wilts, vol XVIII, fo 61.

18 Worsley MSS at Hampshire Record Office (hereafter Hants RO): 16M 48/40.

19 Thynne MSS XVIII, fo 23.

20 Hants RO, 16M 48/41, 42, 45, 63.

21 Masons' Company records, Guildhall Library, London: MS 5313 (Quarterage Book, 1663-95), 8 Jan, 10 Jan 1683/4; 13 Aug 1686; Midsummer 1705, MS 5304/1, fo 72.

22 Hants RO, 16M 48/42-44, 63.

23 *Country Life,* vol 72 (July-Dec 1932), p 571.

24 Thynne MSS XVIII, fo 32.

25 Cf. Kerry Downes, *English Baroque Architecture* (1966), p 67.

26 The details about James, and the quotations in this paragraph, are from H M Colvin, *A Biographical Dictionary of English Architects 1660-1840* (London, 1954).

27 Jane Lang, *Rebuilding St Paul's* (1956), pp 174, 200.

28 Building details in the preceding paragraphs from Hants RO, volumes cited above.

29 John Harris, 'The Building of Denham Place', *Records of Buckinghamshire* (1957-8).

30 Ibid,/40, 63; information from Paul Paget, Esp.

31 See my article 'Sir Richard Worsley and the firm of Chippendale' *The Burlington Magazine,* CX no 783. June 1968, p 352 and figs 43, 44, also my edition of an Appuldurcombe furniture inventory in *Furniture History,* vol i (1965).

32 *Op cit,* p 572.

33 Hoare's Bank Archives, London: Ledger I, fo 136; 8, fo 467.

34 Illustrated in *Furniture History,* i (1965), where it is wrongly attributed to the drawing-room. The *grate* was, in all probability, from the drawing-room.

35 Donn is mentioned at Claydon in articles by Lady Margaret Verney and Patrick Abercrombie in the *Architectural Review* June-Aug (1926); also Christopher Hussey, *English Country Houses: Early Georgian 1715-60* (2nd ed London 1965), 245; the letters from Donn to Verney are at Claydon. I am grateful to Mr Howard Colvin for drawing my attention to the drawing which is also there. The payments by Worsley to Donn are in Hoare's archives; Ledger 89, fo 17; 93, fo 37; 94, fo 265, 266; 96, fo 72, 74, 75; 97, fo 435, 436, 437, 438; 99, fo 250,251, 253; 1, fo 138; 8, fo 466.

36 Sir Richard Worsley, A Catalogue *Raisonné* ... (1804), p 31.

37 W C F G Sheridan, *A Historical and Topographical Guide to the Isle of Wight* (1832), p 168.

Acknowledgements

I am grateful to the Marquess of Bath for allowing me to quote from the Thynne MSS at Longleat, and to the Earl of Yarborough for allowing me to use the Worsley MSS at Lincoln Record Office.

I have greatly benefited from discussion and correspondence with Sir John Summerson, Mr Howard Colvin, Dr Kerry Downes, Mr Paul Paget, P W Montague-Smith, Geoffrey Beard, R G Newbury and J E Cooper.

I am also indebted to Mrs J Varley, archivist of the Lincolnshire Archives Committee, Mrs E Cottrill, Hampshire County Archivist, Mr R Winder, archivist of Hoare's Bank, and to the Department of the Environment for help in various ways.

GLOSSARY

Adam Elegant neo-classical style created by the brothers Robert and James Adam in the eighteenth century

Ashlar Squared, hewn stone laid in regular courses with fine vertical joints

Baroque Style of architecture in Europe of the seventeenth and part of the eighteenth centuries, characterised by extensive ornamentation

Bolection moulding Convex moulding used to cover a joint between two surfaces, projecting beyond both

Buttress Masonry built against a wall to give it additional strength

Capital Head of column or pillar

Cartouche Ornamental panel in the form of a scroll, usually bearing an inscription and sometimes ornately framed

Colonnade Row of columns supporting an entablature

Corinthian One of the three Grecian orders, having bell-shaped capitals with rows of acanthus leaves, and usually fluted columns

Cornice Horizontal moulded projection crowning a building, especially the uppermost part of an entablature

Engaged column Column attached to, or partly sunk into, a wall

Entablature Horizontal part of an order above a column (see diagram)

Frieze Middle division of an entablature, usually decorated

Giant order Order of columns rising from the ground through several storeys

Ha-ha Wall or fence erected in a dip to keep animals out of a park or gardens without obstructing the view

Ice-house Building often wholly or partly underground for storing ice and food

Ionic One of the three Grecian orders, characterised by the two spiral scrolls of its capital

Japanned Lacquered with japan, a hard varnish

Joist One of parallel timbers stretched from wall to wall, to support floor-boards

Keystone Central stone of an arch, sometimes carved

Mansard Roof with a double slope, where the lower is longer and steeper than the upper

Modillion Projecting bracket under top part of cornice in Corinthian and other orders

Neo-classical Formal and restrained style of architecture and decoration, dominant in Europe c.1760-90, inspired by the principles of Greek and Roman architecture

Obelisk Tall tapering shaft of stone

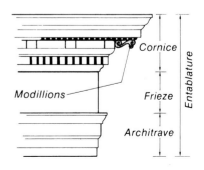

An entablature